THE DARING NELLIE BLY

America's Star Reporter

BONNIE CHRISTENSEN

Alfred A. Knopf
New York

IN 1889

a twenty-five-year-old newspaper reporter had a daring idea.

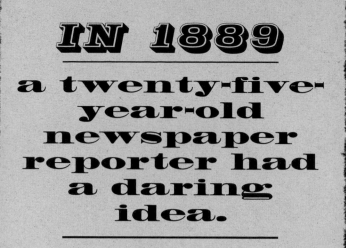

She would travel around the world in less than eighty days. No one had ever traveled so fast—no one except the fictional character Phileas Fogg, from Jules Verne's popular novel *Around the World in Eighty Days.* The young reporter intended to beat him.

Her editor at the *New York World* thought that it was a brilliant idea but said that only a man could succeed.

"Very well," she snapped. "Start the man, and I'll start the same day for some other newspaper and beat him."

That woman was Elizabeth Cochran. The world would come to know her by her pen name, Nellie Bly. In an age when women were not entitled to vote, when few women could attend college, and when fewer held jobs, Nellie Bly dared to defy convention. Her exploits and adventurous spirit changed how the world viewed women and paved the way for the young women who followed.

She was born on May 5, 1864, in Cochran's Mills, Pennsylvania, and grew up competing with two older brothers. Her father, a prosperous and influential judge, was a model of will and determination. From her mother she learned the art of standing out from the crowd. While other little girls dressed in drab browns and grays, Nellie's mother saw to it that she was always turned out in frilly pink frocks.

When Nellie was only six, her father died unexpectedly, and the family fell on hard times. Eventually Mrs. Cochran married again, but her new husband soon proved to be abusive and incapable of supporting the family. When the marriage ended in divorce six years later, Nellie, age fourteen, was called upon to testify at her mother's divorce trial.

During the miserable years of her mother's second marriage, Nellie began realizing that she never wanted to depend on anyone but herself. So when it came time for her to consider marriage, Nellie decided upon a career instead. Teaching, one of the few professions open to women, would allow her to use her head while making her way in the world. But after only one semester at a teachers college, her money ran out.

The Cochrane family moved to the noisy, smoke-blackened city of Pittsburgh when Nellie was sixteen. Her brothers quickly found good white-collar jobs. Jobs for girls and women were plentiful too—in factories and sweatshops. Nellie spent five years looking for work, but there was no suitable position for her.

Then she read an article in the Pittsburgh *Dispatch* that changed her life.

The writer claimed that any woman who had a job was "a monstrosity" and that "in China . . . they kill baby girls or sell them as slaves, because they can make no good use of them."

Nellie was enraged by the article and quickly fired off a letter of protest. Hers was just one in a large pile on the editor's desk, but it caught his eye. The writer spoke her mind with such spirit and conviction, the editor was convinced she had the makings of a top-notch journalist. He invited Nellie for an interview. When she arrived at the *Dispatch* office out of breath, the editor thought she seemed like a "shy little girl." But Nellie spoke her mind, impressed the editor, and won her first newspaper assignment—an extraordinary honor in an age when women journalists reporting serious news were practically unheard of.

She went on to write a long series of startling reports about the hard lives of working girls and women. Then, "determined to do what no girl had done before," she hopped a train to Mexico. The articles Nellie sent home about the lives and customs of the Mexican people proved popular, but her straightforward criticism of the corrupt government angered Mexican officials. Nellie had to flee the country to avoid arrest. Back at the *Dispatch,* she was assigned to report on art and the theater. This was not Nellie's idea of serious news. One day she didn't show up for work. The note she left simply said, "I am off for New York. Look out for me. Bly."

If Nellie thought she would take New York by storm, she was sadly mistaken. Job competition was fierce, and women were considered entirely unsuitable for reporting. After six months of looking for work, her money began running out. More determined than ever, Nellie desperately talked her way into the offices of New York's biggest paper, the *New York World.* She was in the right place at the right time.

The *World* needed an undercover, or "stunt," reporter clever and courageous enough to convince the authorities that she was insane and get herself committed to the Women's Lunatic Asylum at Blackwell's Island. For years there had been rumors of horrendous conditions at the asylum—of brutal beatings, rotten food, and freezing baths. The *World*'s stunt reporter would have to endure these nightmarish conditions for ten days. Then a lawyer would procure her release, and she would write about her experience in a series of articles. Certainly it was a terrifying and dangerous proposition, but Nellie Bly knew it was also an extraordinary opportunity. She accepted.

Nellie's acting skills soon had judges and doctors believing that she was truly insane. Just five days after being offered the *World* assignment, Nellie was condemned to Blackwell's Island. When the asylum doors slammed behind her, she was on her own, without a friend to turn to.

On October 4, 1887, a grateful Nellie was released from the asylum as planned, already composing in her head the exposé that would blaze across the *World*'s front page.

Nellie's scoop on the Blackwell's Island asylum made her famous as the first female stunt reporter and led to improved conditions in New York's asylums. She followed with exposés on unfair and illegal practices affecting the lives of ordinary women. Soon Nellie Bly was the *World*'s star stunt reporter, responsible for coming up with her own great story ideas.

THE WORLD.

INSIDE THE MADHOUSE

Nellie Bly's Experience in the Blackwell's Island Asylum.

Continuation of the Story of Ten Days With Lunatics.

How the City's Unfortunate Wards Are Fed and Treated.

The Terrors of Cold Baths and Cruel Unsympathetic Nurses.

Attendants Who Harass and Abuse Patients and Laugh at Their Miseries.

One sleepless night she had an extraordinary idea. She would break the fictional record of Phileas Fogg, who went around the world in eighty days in Jules Verne's popular novel.

In the late 1800s it took many months to travel around the world. Boats were late, trains were slow, and connections were often missed. But Nellie checked the timetables and was convinced she could beat Fogg's record. Her editor was doubtful. A woman could not travel without a chaperone, he argued, and transferring her dozens of trunks would cause missed connections.

But Nellie was determined—she didn't need a chaperone and could travel with only one piece of hand luggage. Besides, if the *World* wouldn't send her, she'd simply find another newspaper that would. Finally her editor relented. The question was: Could she start her journey in two days?

The short notice didn't faze Nellie a bit. She visited a dressmaker and ordered a dress that would stand constant wear for three months. Then she bought a long, loose coat and one handbag, 16" x 7", into which she would squeeze all her essentials.

For Nellie Bly the clock began ticking at 9:40 A.M., November 14, 1889, when her ship, the *Augusta Victoria,* steamed away from its pier in **HOBOKEN, NEW JERSEY.** She had been warned of intense heat, bitter cold, terrible storms, shipwrecks, and fevers, but her greatest fear was failure. She said she'd rather return dead than "alive and behind time." Along the route she would cable stories back to the *World,* sharing with her readers rare glimpses into life on the other side of the globe.

No sooner had the *Augusta Victoria* left harbor than Bly was confronted with her first challenge—overcoming seasickness.

"And *she's* going around the world!" one man sneered. But Nellie's motto was "Energy rightly applied and directed will accomplish anything." By the time she arrived in Southampton, England, she had conquered her seasickness and was in good spirits.

From **SOUTHAMPTON** Nellie made a quick side trip to **AMIENS, FRANCE,** to meet Jules Verne. Together they charted her journey on the map Verne had used to outline Phileas Fogg's route. Then, worried about missing her train to **BRINDISI, ITALY,** Nellie departed.

The trip through France and Italy was dark, cold, and foggy. When the train arrived at Brindisi two hours late, Nellie feared her ship, the *Victoria,* had sailed without her. Luckily, it was still in port, so on she traveled without delay. On through the **SUEZ CANAL** to **ADEN, YEMEN.**

A shipboard friend told Nellie it was rumored she was "an eccentric American heiress, traveling about with a hairbrush and a bankbook."

Nellie reached **COLOMBO, CEYLON** (now Sri Lanka), two days ahead of schedule; then her luck ran out. Her next ship, the *Oriental*, was delayed five days. Any more delays between Colombo and Hong Kong would mean losing her race. Nellie lost patience when an elderly gentleman suggested that Colombo was a pleasant place to stay. "It may be," she exclaimed, "if staying there does not mean more than life to one!"

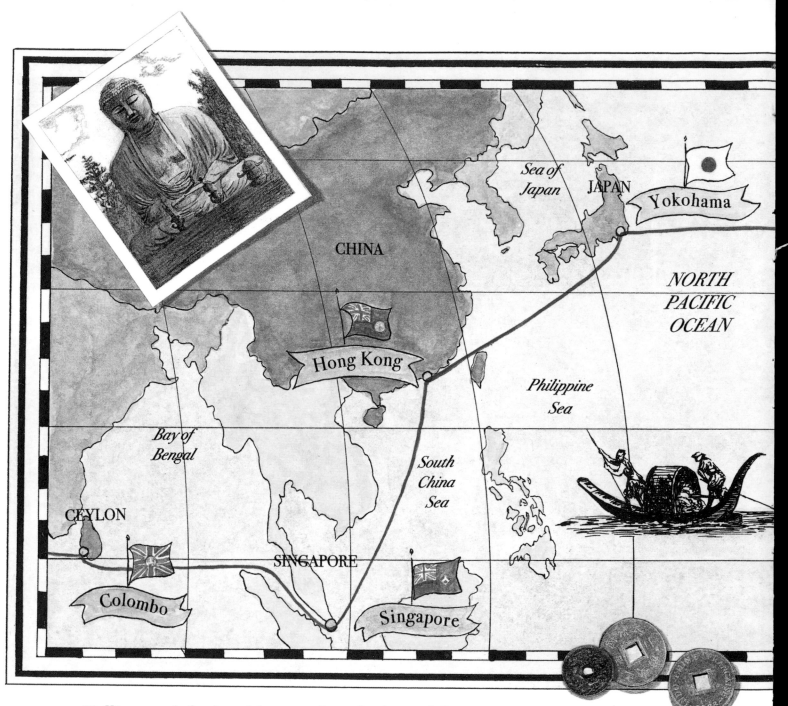

Nellie was infuriated by another daylong delay in **SINGAPORE,** which she feared would seal her doom. That night she endured agonies of "suspense and impatience." The next day she toured the city, though, and bought a monkey, whom she named McGinty.

When her ship finally sailed, it was wracked by raging monsoons, which at one point filled Nellie's cabin with water. Against all odds, they arrived two days early in **HONG KONG.** Nellie was thrilled. It was the thirty-ninth day of her journey and she'd traveled halfway around the world.

Then, at the steamship company, a man informed Nellie that she had a competitor. Reporter Elizabeth Bisland had been sent by a magazine to beat Nellie's time, and it looked like she would succeed. Nellie was further disheartened to learn that her own ship, the *Oceanic,* would be delayed five days before sailing to Japan.

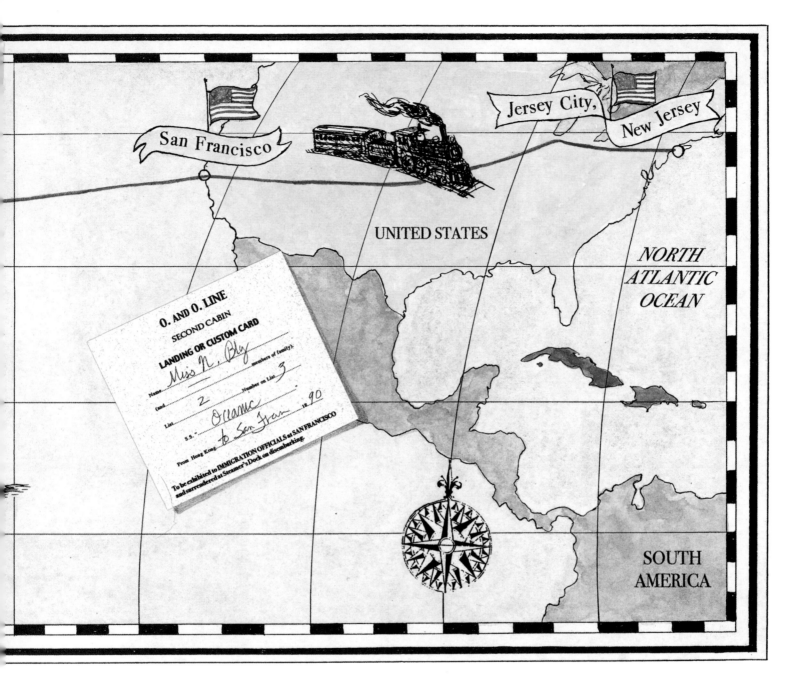

On January 7 the *Oceanic* began the Pacific crossing from **YOKOHAMA, JAPAN,** to San Francisco. Nellie had an ocean and a continent to cross—8,000 miles—and only twenty-five days in which to do it. Everyone on board knew Nellie's story, and everyone was rooting for her. The ship's chief engineer had emblazoned across the engines, "For Nellie Bly, we'll win or die."

Thirteen days later **SAN FRANCISCO** was in sight, but there was more troubling news. The worst snowstorm in ten years had hit the Northwest. The planned train route was impassable. The *World* decided to hire a special train to take a southerly route cross-country. All along the way Nellie was greeted by crowds of well-wishers, bands, and fireworks. Telegrams, flowers, fruit, and candy poured in.

On January 25, 1890—seventy-two days, six hours, and eleven minutes after the start of her journey—Nellie Bly set foot in the Jersey City train station. A huge, cheering throng greeted her. Cannons roared. "The American girl will no longer be misunderstood," declared the mayor. "She will be recognized as pushing and determined, independent, able to take care of herself wherever she may go." Nellie Bly had won much more than her race against the clock.

Nellie's exploit increased the *World*'s circulation by 24,000. The newspaper described her as "the best known and most widely talked of young woman on earth today." It wasn't an exaggeration. Her picture appeared on games, toys, cigars, soaps, and medicines. A racehorse, hotel, and train were named after her. The name Nellie Bly was heard and recognized everywhere.

Throughout her life Nellie Bly continued to campaign for the rights of women and the working class. In 1895 she married Robert Seaman, a wealthy industrialist, and when he died, she successfully ran his huge manufacturing company as a model of social welfare. She invented the first steel barrel and held patents for twenty-five other inventions.

During World War I, Nellie Bly, at fifty, was the first woman journalist to report from the Eastern Front. After the war she returned to New York City, where she wrote a column for the *New York Journal* and crusaded tirelessly to find permanent homes for orphans.

Although she was in and out of the hospital from exhaustion, Nellie Bly continued her work, writing that each individual has a moral responsibility to "the whole wide world of mankind: good, bad and indifferent."

When Nellie Bly died on January 27, 1922, her friend and editor Arthur Brisbane dedicated an entire column to her. "She was the best reporter in America," he wrote. ". . . She takes with her from this earth all that she cared for, an honorable name, the respect and affection of her fellow workers, the memory of good fights well fought and of many good deeds never to be forgotten by those who had no friend but Nellie Bly."

CHRONOLOGY OF
NELLIE BLY

May 5, 1864 Born to Judge Michael and Mary Jane Cochran in Cochran's Mills, Pennsylvania. Christened Elizabeth Jane Cochran.

July 1870 Father dies. His estate is divided among many heirs.

September 1879 Begins teacher training at Indiana Normal School, in Indiana, Pennsylvania. Attends for one term.

1880 Moves to Pittsburgh, Pennsylvania, with her family. The Cochranes begin using an *e* at the end of their name.

January 1885 Hired as a full-time reporter by the Pittsburgh *Dispatch*. Adopts pseudonym Nellie Bly.

1886 Travels to Mexico. Sends news stories back to the *Dispatch*. Publishes book, *Six Months in Mexico*.

1887 Moves to New York City and is hired by Joseph Pulitzer's *New York World*. Publishes *Ten Days in a Madhouse,* recounting her experience at New York's insane asylum on Blackwell's Island.

November 14, 1889–January 25, 1890 Travels around the world in record-breaking time. A few weeks later quits the *World* in a huff.

1893 Rejoins the *World*. Writes high-profile interviews and exposés.

1894 Covers notorious Pullman strike in Chicago. Only reporter sympathetic to strikers and their cause.

1895 Marries millionaire businessman Robert L. Seaman.

1904 Seaman dies. Bly takes over running his manufacturing companies.

August 1914 Travels to Austria. Becomes the first woman war correspondent on the Eastern Front in World War I.

1919 Returns to New York. Writes for the *New York Journal*. Takes up cause of orphaned and abandoned children.

January 27, 1922 Dies of pneumonia in New York.

✑ Bibliography ✑

Freeden, Charles. *Nellie Bly: Daredevil Reporter*. Minneapolis, Minn.: Lerner Publications Company, 2000.

Kendall, Martha. *Nellie Bly: Reporter for the <u>World</u>*. Brookfield, Conn.: Millbrook Press, 1992.

Kroeger, Brooke. *Nellie Bly: Daredevil, Reporter, Feminist*. New York: Times Books, Random House, 1994.

Peck, Ira, ed. *Nellie Bly's Book <u>Around the World in 72 Days</u>* (abridged). Brookfield, Conn.: Twenty First Century Books, 1998.

Verne, Jules. *Around the World in Eighty Days* (abridged), trans. William Butcher. New York: Oxford University Press, 1995.

✑ Videography ✑

Around the World in 72 Days. New York: The American Experience, PBS Home Video, 1997.

For Leslie

*Special thanks to Emily Herder, Ginny Joyner, Luci Stein,
and Catherine Wood Brooks and the Shelburne Museum,
Shelburne, Vermont*

Library of Congress Cataloging-in-Publication Data
Christensen, Bonnie.
The daring Nellie Bly / by Bonnie Christensen.
p.   cm.
SUMMARY: Introduces the life of Nellie Bly, who, as a "stunt reporter" for the *New York World*
newspaper in the late 1800s, championed women's rights and traveled around the world
faster than anyone ever had. Includes bibliographical references.
ISBN 0-375-81568-6 (trade) — ISBN 0-375-91568-0 (lib. bdg.)
1. Nellie Bly, 1864–1922—Juvenile literature. 2. Journalists—United States—Biography—
Juvenile literature. [1. Bly, Nellie, 1864–1922. 2. Journalists. 3. Women—Biography.] I. Title.
PN4874.C59C49 2003
070.92—dc21
2002152478

Printed in the United States of America
October 2003
10 9 8 7 6 5 4 3 2
First Edition